DATE DUE

MAR 1 1 2003	
GAYLORD	PRINTED IN U.S.A.

Puerto Rico

JoAnn Milivojevic

 Carolrhoda Books, Inc. / Minneapolis

Photo Acknowledgments

Photos, maps, and artworks are used courtesy of: John Erste, pp. 1, 2–3, 6–7, 13, 25, 26–27, 39; Laura Westlund, pp. 4–5, 37; © Mark Bacon, pp. 6, 7 (both), 8–9, 10, 13, 19 (top), 21 (left), 29 (right), 30 (both), 31, 36, 40 (both), 41, 43 (left); © Eugene Schulz, p. 9 (top); © Thomas R. Fletcher, pp. 9 (bottom), 19 (bottom); © Jaime Santiago/D. Donne Bryant Stock Photo, p. 11 (top); © Suzanne Murphy-Larronde/DDB Stock Photo, pp. 11 (bottom), 16 (both), 25; Knights of Columbus Headquarters Museum, p. 12; Puerto Rico General Archives, p. 14; © Richard B. Levine, p. 17; © Robert Fried, pp. 18, 27, 26, 34, 34–35, 37, 38, 45; © Tony Arruza, pp. 20, 22, 24; © D. Donne Bryant/DDB Stock Photo, p. 21 (right); © TRIP/R. C. Fournier, p. 23; Bob Krist/The Puerto Rico Tourism Co., pp. 28, 29 (left), 39; © Joan Iaconetti, pp. 32, 42, 43 (right); © W. Lynn Seldon Jr./DDB Stock Photo, p. 33; Pittsburgh Pirates, p. 35; Cover photo of handmade masks by © Suzanne Murphy-Larronde/DDB Stock Photo.

Carolrhoda Books, Inc.
A Division of Lerner Publishing Group
241 First Avenue North
Minneapolis, Minnesota 55401 U.S.A.

Website address: www.lernerbooks.com

Words in **bold type** are explained in a glossary that begins on page 44.

Library of Congress Cataloging-in-Publication Data

Milivojevic, JoAnn
    Puerto Rico / by JoAnn Milivojevic.
        p. cm. — (Globetrotter's club)
    Includes index.
    Summary: Examines the history, geography, society, economy, and culture of Puerto Rico.
        ISBN 1–57505–119–2 (lib. bdg. : alk. paper)
        1. Puerto Rico—Juvenile literature. [1. Puerto Rico.] I. Title. II. Series: Globe-trotters club (Series)
F1958.3.M56 2000   98–54648
972.95—dc21

Manufactured in the United States of America
1 2 3 4 5 6 – JR – 05 04 03 02 01 00

Contents

UNITED STATES

Florida

¡*Bienvenidos al*
Puerto Rico!*

*That's "Welcome to Puerto Rico" in Spanish,
the official language of Puerto Rico.*

 Travel 1,000 miles southeast from Florida, and you'll end up in Puerto Rico. The **U.S. commonwealth** of Puerto Rico is surrounded by water. The rough Atlantic Ocean splashes its northern coast. The warm Caribbean Sea laps the southern shore. The Atlantic and Caribbean waters mingle on the eastern and western coasts. The Commonwealth of Puerto Rico includes three small islands—Vieques, Culebra, and Mona—and one large island named Puerto Rico. The commonwealth is part of a Caribbean island group called the West Indies. Puerto Rico's neighbors to the west are Haiti and the Dominican Republic (which share the island of Hispaniola). To the east sit the Virgin Islands.

Fast Facts about Puerto Rico

Official Name: Estado Libre Asociado de Puerto Rico (Commonwealth of Puerto Rico)

Area: 3,515 square miles

Main Landforms: Cordillera Central, Sierra de Luquillo, Arecibo River, La Plata River

Highest Point: Cerro de Punta (4,389 feet)

Lowest Point: Sea level

Animals: Frogs, Puerto Rican parrots, lizards, hummingbirds, sea turtles, iguanas, bats

Capital City: San Juan

Other Major Cities: Bayamón, Ponce, Carolina, Caguas, Mayagüez, Arecibo

Official Language: Spanish

Money Unit: U.S. dollar (called peso in Puerto Rico)

Port of San Juan

San Juan

Loíza

Arecibo

PUERTO RICO

Arecibo River

La Plata River

Bayamón

Carolina

El Yunque

SIERRA DE LUQUILLO

Mayagüez

Cerro de Punta

Caguas

N

C O R D I L L E R A   C E N T R A L

Ponce

Guayama

Miles
0   10   20
0   10   20   30
Kilometers

	mountains
	foothills
	karst
	lowlands
	semidesert
	rain forest
★	capital city

A T L A N T I C
O C E A N

I

N

D

I

E

S

VIRGIN ISLANDS

HAITI

DOMINICAN REPUBLIC

Culebra

Puerto Rico

H I S P A N I O L A

Mona

Vieques

COMMONWEALTH OF PUERTO RICO

C A R I B B E A N   S E A

5

A boat noses through the waters of a mangrove forest in Puerto Rico. Much of a mangrove tree's root system grows aboveground.

Sandy Shores
and More

Sandy beaches and hidden **coves** ring Puerto Rico. The tangled roots of **mangrove** trees grow along the shores in muddy, saltwater areas. Their long, thin trunks look like bony fingers grabbing at the sea. Along Puerto Rico's northern coast, rainy lowlands are lush with life. Grasses, bushes, trees, and other plants grow tall and close together. Farmers there grow sugarcane and pineapples.

Lumpy hills and mysterious pits in the north make the country-side look like a moonscape. Over thousands of years, underground streams have worn away the lime-stone (a soft rock), leaving behind caves, hills, and craters. This land-scape is called karst.

Is Anybody out There?

In the karst country of northern Puerto Rico sits the Arecibo Observatory. It has the largest radio-radar telescope on earth. Space lovers can get a terrific look at outer space from there. The 1,000-foot-wide telescope sits in a 565-foot-deep crater. Scientists at the observatory study the earth's atmosphere—and search for aliens.

The mysterious landscape in northwestern Puerto Rico might stop visitors in their tracks.

Moving inland, slanting **foothills** give way to the towering mountains of the Cordillera Central, which runs from west to east through the middle of the island. Coffee farms cling to steep mountainsides. The Sierra de Luquillo mountain range in the northeast gets rain nearly every day. But head to the southwestern side and you'll find prickly cactus living in the **semidesert,** where only 40 inches of rain fall each year.

Wet and **Wild**

Puerto Rico stays warm—82 degrees on average—all year. Ocean breezes help cool things down. But sometimes those winds whip into high speeds. **Hurricanes** (tropical storms) can batter Puerto Rico, causing much damage.

Lots of rain and warm weather make the perfect conditions for **tropical rain forests.** Puerto Rico's rain forest, called El Yunque, gets more than 100 billion gallons of rain every year. Trees reach heights of more than 100 feet! Gazing up at the thick tangle of leaves is like looking at the sky through a piece of lace.

Plants cling, climb, hang, and twist through the moist air. All those plants make great homes for tons of rain forest animals. A rain forest is like a high-rise apartment building. Some creatures that live in the canopy (tops of the trees) may never meet their downstairs neighbors. Others that live in the middle and ground floors may never visit the treetops.

In 1989 Hurricane Hugo struck Puerto Rico. Over the years, Puerto Ricans have survived hundreds of these storms.

Sunlight filters through the trees of El Yunque. About 240 different kinds of trees and flowers grow in the rain forest.

Puerto Rican Mascot

As night falls, rain forest creatures whistle, click, and snap. Among the sounds, you'll hear "koh-KEE, koh-KEE!" That's *el coquí*, a small, yellowish tree frog about the size of your pinky finger. El coquí loves to sing its sweet song at sunset. Puerto Ricans adore this cute little frog. Its image appears on T-shirts, key chains, and postcards.

A Taino adult shows his young friend how to build a tool by hand. At historical parks, visitors to modern-day Puerto Rico can see how the Taino Indians once lived.

Island of the
Brave Lord

Some of the first people to live in Puerto Rico were the Taino Indians. They called their island Borinquén, meaning "Island of the Brave Lord." The Tainos farmed, growing yams, maize (corn), beans, squash, and a starchy root called manioc. They speared and netted fish in the abundant sea and hunted small animals, such as wild pigeons and parrots.

Taino traders paddled canoes to many nearby islands and visited other native groups. They swapped handmade goods as well as languages and customs. The Tainos carved wooden bowls, boxes, and tools. They crafted large wooden thrones for their rulers and wove cotton into cloth for clothing, belts, and hammocks. Artisans made pottery for cooking and for decoration.

The Tainos built their homes on tall center poles to keep air flowing through the rooms on hot nights.

The Tainos spent their days outdoors but slept in airy homes at night. They constructed houses with roofs of thatched wood and leaves. The Tainos built the roofs of these houses on tall poles. Breezes blew through the home, keeping sleepers cool on hot nights. As many as 40 people slept in one large house!

An Old Game

The Tainos built villages around large public squares called *bayetes*. There they held festivals and dances and played a ritual ball game similar to modern-day soccer. The ball court was lined with stone. Players could not touch the ball with their hands. They wore stone belts on their waists to deflect the ball. Historians believe the game got its start as far away as Mexico.

The Tainos welcomed Christopher Columbus and the first Spaniards (left). **But after living under years of harsh rule, the Tainos turned against the Spanish settlers.**

The **Spaniards**

The European explorer Christopher Columbus and his crew arrived on Borinquén in 1493. They claimed the island for Spain and named it San Juan Bautista in honor of a Roman Catholic saint. The Tainos greeted the Spaniards warmly.

The Tainos' attractive villages and beautiful pottery impressed the newcomers, who told of what they saw when they returned to Europe. But the Spaniards most admired the Tainos' gold jewelry and hoped to find more riches on the island. In 1508 Spanish settlers returned to the island in search of the valuable metal. They set up gold-mining operations and forced the Tainos to work in the mines as slaves. Many Tainos died from European diseases, which their bodies couldn't fight. Others fled the island to avoid slavery.

The mines soon ran out of gold, so the Spaniards turned to farming

A Taino potter makes ceramics in much the same way her ancestors did when Columbus visited.

sugarcane, coffee, and tobacco. The crops grew well in Puerto Rico's climate and rich soil. Taino slaves worked hard in the fields. Spanish traders sold the goods to buyers in Europe. When most Tainos had died or left the island, the Spaniards brought slaves from Africa to do the difficult farmwork.

Map Mix-up

The first Spanish settlement on San Juan Bautista was named Caparra. But most Spaniards called the city Puerto Rico, meaning "rich port" in the Spanish language. Historians believe that an early mapmaker switched the names, and the island became known as Puerto Rico, while the town was called San Juan.

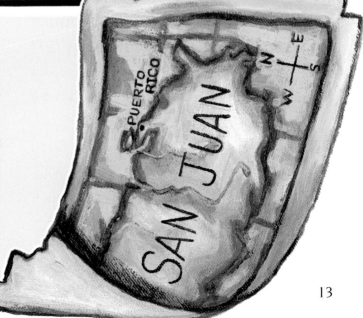

Whose Island Is It?

In the 1500s, Puerto Rico was a hot spot. Famous for its riches and farmland, the island drew many fortune seekers. Its great location as a stopover to other Caribbean islands made it popular among the region's sailors. Pirates and traders eyed Spain's claim. For many years, Puerto Ricans lived through foreign attacks.

Under Spanish rule, cities sprang up, and farming and trading grew. But Spanish rulers imposed harsh laws that turned most Puerto Ricans against Spain. By the 1850s, the islanders demanded more freedom. Spain, weakened by wars, gave Puerto Rico some independence and outlawed slavery in 1873. But Puerto Ricans wanted total control of their homeland. They got their wish in May 1898, when Luis Muñoz

Luis Muñoz Rivera served as Puerto Rico's president for only six months before the United States took over the island.

Rivera became the first leader of independent Puerto Rico. But in the same year, Spain lost a war with the United States. In a deal between Spain and the United States, Puerto Rico fell into U.S. hands. In 1952 the island officially became a U.S. commonwealth.

What's a Commonwealth?

As a U.S. commonwealth, Puerto Ricans have a special relationship with the United States. Puerto Ricans can travel freely to the United States. They can vote to elect the governor of Puerto Rico, but not the U.S. president. Puerto Ricans use U.S. money and have to follow certain U.S. laws, but they don't pay taxes to the United States.

The Puerto Rican flag has the same colors as the American flag.

Many Puerto Ricans are happy with this arrangement. They feel it benefits their country, while they still keep a bit of independence. Other folks would prefer total independence and for Puerto Ricans to govern their own land. Still others would rather that Puerto Rico become a U.S. state. Every so often, the islanders hold a vote to decide how they should be ruled. In an election in 1998, Puerto Rico voted to remain a commonwealth.

Who's **Puerto Rican**

Throughout Puerto Rico, faces range in color from rich cocoa to light copper. Where do all of the beautiful skin tones come from? They are living history. The early Spanish settlers married Taino and African people.

The **descendants** of these marriages became the Puerto Rican people. High cheekbones and deep eyes reveal Taino roots. People with darker skin have African **ancestors.** Blond hair and blue eyes show up in people of Spanish background. Most folks claim relatives from all three **ethnic groups.**

Most Puerto Ricans have ancestors from one or more of Puerto Rico's three main ethnic groups.

16

Of Beauty They Sing

Although Puerto Ricans sing the U.S. national anthem, "The Star Spangled Banner," the island has its own national song. In "La Borinqueña" singers praise the island's beauty.

The land of Borinquén
where I was born
is a flowering garden
of exquisite magic.

A sky, always clear,
serves as its canopy
and sings calm lullabies
to the waves at its feet.

When Columbus came
to its beaches,
he exclaimed, full of admiration,
"Oh! Oh! Oh!

This is the beautiful land
I've been looking for;
it's Borinquén, the daughter,
the daughter of the sea and the sun."

Nuyoricans show their pride during the Puerto Rican Day parade in New York City.

Puerto Ricans are proud of their homeland. Although the country officially belongs to the United States, the people consider themselves Puerto Rican first and U.S. citizens second. But many people move from Puerto Rico to the United States in search of jobs or to go to school. Puerto Ricans in the United States keep close ties with their island home, and many move back later on.

17

High-rise buildings dot the skyline of downtown San Juan.

City **Living**

San Juan, the Puerto Rican capital city, bustles with life. Buses, taxis, and cars whiz through the streets. Shopping malls and parks line the neat cement sidewalks. Tall office buildings share the skyline with high-rise luxury hotels.

Nearly one million people call San Juan home. Most city people live in modern, single-family houses or in apartment buildings. Television sets, radios, and computers are found in most homes.

Many Puerto Ricans in San Juan hold government jobs. They deliver mail, police the streets, or teach classes. Others work in office buildings or sell goods in stores. Many tourists visit Puerto Rico each year, creating lots of jobs in hotels and restaurants. Hundreds of ships dock at the Port of San Juan, which means even more jobs in San Juan.

18

San Juan's citizens couldn't easily forget their Taino, African, and Spanish roots. For example, historic Spanish buildings line the streets of Old San Juan. And city dwellers can munch on food made of beans, corn, and sweet potatoes, once grown by Taino Indians. African rhythms spice up Puerto Rican music. Many of the city's festivals and parades reflect the different cultures that have influenced Puerto Rico.

Carnival, a Roman Catholic holiday, offers folks a chance to parade down the streets dressed in crazy costumes.

Old San Juan

Old San Juan, a seven-block-square area of San Juan, looks like a typical old Spanish town. Antique cathedrals, flower-filled plazas, and lovely cobblestone streets make visitors feel like they've stepped back into another century. Many Puerto Ricans visit the old town to see museums, enjoy the elegant architecture, and shop in the many fine stores.

Country **Living**

Country life is usually more relaxed than the fast-paced city life. In the coastal valleys, many people farm and raise cattle. Farmers grow food for the family to eat. They sell their extra produce at outdoor markets. Other farmers earn money by working on coffee and sugarcane **plantations** owned by the government or by large companies. Country folks generally earn less money than city people do. But country living is less expensive than city life.

In their spare time, people in the country enjoy meeting with friends and neighbors at the *colmado* (village store). Sure, people shop there, but

A farmer picks green peppers near his home in the countryside. His white clothing and hat help keep him cool in the blazing Puerto Rican sun.

Country dwellers pass an afternoon playing dominoes in front of a colmado.

El Jíbaro

Early rural farmers were known as *jíbaros*. Many trace their roots to Taino and African slaves or to Spaniards who chose life in the countryside. Few jíbaros went to school. They worked the land like their parents and grandparents, farming by hand and using horse-drawn plows. The jíbaro's family ate what they grew and sold extra crops at open-air markets in towns. Traditional jíbaro outfits for men included straw hats, white shirts, and loose pants. Women wore colorful skirts and blouses and lots of bright jewelry. These days few people choose to live as jíbaros. But for many Puerto Ricans, the jíbaro represents a simple, independent lifestyle.

the store is like a community center, too. Neighbors gather for a cool drink and to share news of their lives. Men play games of dominoes. At the end of the day, folks head home to small, wooden homes. Families of six or more people usually share one dwelling.

Dad checks the grill during a fun family outing at the beach.

We Are Family

In the countryside, Puerto Rican parents might raise six or more children. They often live under the same roof as grandparents, aunts, uncles, and cousins. Large **extended families** help share the load of farming, cooking, and cleaning. And families care for older family members.

Puerto Rican culture stresses love and respect for elders. For example, children honor adults by calling them "Don" Carlos or "Doña" María. It is like calling somebody "sir" or "madam." Kids are expected to obey older folks and to take their advice seriously. In return, kids always have someone to rely on.

All in the Family

Here are the Spanish words for family members. Practice using these terms on your own family. See if they can understand you!

grandfather	*abuelo*	(ah-BWAY-loh)
grandmother	*abuela*	(ah-BWAY-lah)
father	*papi*	(PAH-pee)
mother	*mami*	(MAH-mee)
uncle	*tío*	(TEE-oh)
aunt	*tía*	(TEE-ah)
son	*hijo*	(EE-hoh)
daughter	*hija*	(EE-hah)
brother	*hermano*	(ehr-MAH-noh)
sister	*hermana*	(ehr-MAH-nah)

City folks often decide to have fewer children. But no matter how big the family, togetherness is important in Puerto Rico. Puerto Rican families like spending time with one another. They go to the countryside or out for dinner. On weekends parents play with their kids at the beach or have a barbecue in the park.

Saints and **Celebrations**

A parade honoring Saint James, the patron saint of Loíza, makes its way across town. Most Puerto Rican towns have their own patron saints.

The Roman Catholic religion, brought from Spain, has a strong following in Puerto Rico. The Baptist, Methodist, Lutheran, and Episcopalian branches of Christianity have many believers as well. Some Puerto Ricans practice *espiritismo*, or "spiritualism," which blends Taino, African, and Catholic religious beliefs.

Most island celebrations are based on Catholic holidays. Every town has a patron saint, who is believed to watch over and to protect the townspeople. Everybody turns out to honor the saint on special days with music, dancing, lots of food, and ceremonies. The festivities can last up to 10 days. Saint John the Baptist is the patron saint

Troubles Fly Away

Followers of espiritismo believe that certain rituals help attract good spirits, while others help get rid of bad spirits. A very special espiritismo ritual is used to greet the new year. Just before midnight on New Year's Eve, the abuela (grandmother) holds a live white dove by the feet. She sweeps it across the fronts and backs of all family members. Believers feel that the bird absorbs their worries. The eldest son releases the bird outside. The dove flies away, carrying all the family's problems with it, and the new year begins fresh.

of San Juan. At midnight on June 23, people walk backward into the ocean three times. Puerto Ricans believe that the ritual renews good luck for the coming year.

Christmastime is also special in Puerto Rico. Instead of receiving gifts on Christmas Day, kids open presents on Three Kings' Day (January 6). In the Christian tradition, three wise kings reached the baby Jesus on that day. When they found him, they gave gifts. On the night of January 5, kids place grass under their beds as a snack for the kings' camels. The next morning, the grass is gone, but in its place are presents.

These kids act out the Christian story of the three wise men on Three Kings' Day.

¿Habla Español?

That means "Do you speak Spanish?" Although Puerto Ricans are U.S. citizens, their official language is Spanish. People speak it at home, to their friends and neighbors, and on the street. Puerto Rican Spanish is a blend of Spanish, English, and Taino. Words like *hamaca* (hammock), *tabaco* (tobacco), *canoa* (canoe), and *barbacoa* (barbecue) originally came from the Tainos.

All street signs are printed in Spanish, the official language of Puerto Rico.

Sidetrack
The word *hurricane* comes from the Taino name Juracán, meaning "God of the Fierce Winds." In Spanish the *j* is pronounced as an *h*, so you get *huracán* (hurricane).

26

More and more Puerto Ricans can speak both Spanish and English. These folks are **bilingual,** meaning they can speak two languages. Kids learn English in school. It is the language of business and of the tourist industry. Many people from the United States do business in Puerto Rico or travel there for fun in the sun.

Nuyoricans have invented their own brand of Spanish. Called "Spanglish," it's a blend of Spanish, English, and New York City street talk. For example, *liders* means "leaders." P*oquete* is "pocket," like those found on a pool table. What do you suppose *elevador* means? That's right, "elevator"! And the grassy plot of land around a house is a *yarda*, or "yard." Many of these new words have made their way to Puerto Rico, too.

Most signs in places through which U.S. travelers might pass are printed in both Spanish and English.

All Passengers Traveling To The U.S. Mainland Must Present Their Baggage For Inspection By U.S. Agriculture.

Todo Pasajero Que Viaja A Los E.U. Continentales Debe Presentar Su Equipaje Para Inspeccion De Agricultura Federal.

Still **Standing**

In Puerto Rico, tall, modern buildings tower next to historic Spanish structures. Some of these sturdy buildings are hundreds of years old. Built in 1522, La Fortaleza, located in San Juan, is the oldest government mansion in the Western **Hemisphere.** It's the home of Puerto Rico's governor—the island's highest elected official.

The citizens of Ponce take great pride in their city, calling it *la perla del sur* (the pearl of the south). Residents take special care of the old buildings. They preserve unique features that were once practical.

La Fortaleza in San Juan looks like a royal castle. La Fortaleza means "the fortress" in Spanish.

An example of buildings with rounded corners in Ponce

For example, buildings on street corners have rounded edges instead of sharp corners. Before cars became popular, people traveled by horse and buggy. In a horse-drawn carriage, it was much easier to steer around a curve than to turn a sharp corner. These days tourists can hitch a ride on a horse-drawn carriage.

El Morro

In Puerto Rico's early years, the Spaniards built a fortress in San Juan to protect the island from frequent attacks by the region's traders and pirates. They named it El Morro. Finished in 1540, the sturdy fortress towers 140 feet above the sea. Its strong walls are nearly 20 feet thick. No cannonball could ever get through El Morro. Inside the fortress lurk secret tunnels, scary dungeons, and rooms for soldiers. But the Spaniards wanted even more protection. In 1783 builders completed a wall that enclosed the entire city of San Juan.

Getting **Hungry?**

City people shop in large, air-conditioned supermarkets and at smaller, open-air markets that carry fresh produce. A typical shopping list includes beans, rice, plantains (large, starchy bananas), meat, coffee, eggs, and fruit.

Before going to school, Puerto Rican kids eat a hearty breakfast of scrambled eggs, sausage, or French toast. Adults savor cups of delicious coffee made from beans grown right on the island. A favorite dinner item is *asopao*, a delicious slow-simmered stew made with vegetables, meat or fish, and rice. A side of *tostones* (fried plantains) makes the meal complete.

Many delicious fruits and vegetables grow in Puerto Rico's rich soil. Unusual tropical fruits abound.

Fruit at an open-air market (left) **looks lip-smacking good. Tostones** (above) **are a Puerto Rican favorite.**

Mango Smoothie

For a cool, mango-flavored treat, try this smoothie on a hot summer day. Have an adult help you with the cutting.

You will need:

1 firm, ripe mango	1¼ cup orange juice
1 banana	a blender

1. To cut the mango fruit away from the seed, slice the fruit down each side of the pit, about half an inch from an imaginary line down the center. Try to cut as close to the seed as possible.
2. Place the two sides on a cutting board with the skin side facedown. Using the tip of the knife, cut lengthwise and crosswise through the flesh, being careful not to cut through the skin. Pick up each piece and push on the skin side as if to turn it inside out. You'll easily be able to pick off chunks of mango. Carefully slice away the rest of the flesh from the seed and then cut off the skin.
3. Slice a peeled banana into chunks and put it with the mango into a plastic container or freezer bag. Freeze the fruit overnight.
4. In a blender, combine the orange juice, frozen banana, and frozen mango chunks. Blend until smooth and pour into a tall glass.

You've probably eaten bananas and coconuts, but what about a *genip*? It looks like a large grape and has a tough outer skin. The inside is a mushy, sweet, melt-in-your-mouth treat. Mangoes are popular desserts in Puerto Rico. About the size of softballs, they fall like raindrops from the trees as they ripen. Even horses eat mangoes in Puerto Rico!

All aboard this colorful schoolbus.

School **Days**

In Puerto Rico, kids wear uniforms to school. Each school has its own school colors and style of uniform. Girls usually wear a jumper, a blouse, and black or brown shoes with white socks. Until third grade, boys wear short pants and a polo shirt. Older boys wear long pants.

Classes might have as many as 30 to 40 students in one classroom. Beginning in kindergarten, most kids learn to speak English. History is a very important subject to Puerto Ricans. Students learn about their island home and take field trips to Spanish forts in San Juan. Kids take classes in art, music, computers, and gym. Physical activities include volleyball, basketball, baseball, running, and the long jump. During recess students play games such as jacks, or they jump rope.

Count in Spanish

one	*uno*	(OO-noh)
two	*dos*	(DOHS)
three	*tres*	(TRAYS)
four	*cuatro*	(KWAH-troh)
five	*cinco*	(SEEN-koh)
six	*seis*	(SAYSS)
seven	*siete*	(SYAY-tay)
eight	*ocho*	(OH-choh)
nine	*nueve*	(NWAY-vay)
ten	*diez*	(DYAYS)

Schoolkids pose for a photo with their teacher during a field trip in Ponce.

Batter **Up!**

Chalk diamonds, wooden bats, and leather gloves can mean only one thing—baseball. Nearly every major city in Puerto Rico has an official team. Watching television at home or sitting in seats in the bleachers, Puerto Rican fans can see a ballgame almost every day. Puerto Rican athletes excel at the sport. Some Puerto Rican baseball players swing, run, and catch for major-league teams in the United States.

Many kids dribble, shoot, and score in a game of basketball. Friends gather for games on weekends, and most schools have basketball teams, too. Both parents and kids enjoy playing golf and tennis.

The game of basketball is becoming more and more popular among Puerto Rico's athletes.

Step up to the plate! Baseball is still Puerto Ricans' favorite sport.

Athlete with a Cause

Puerto Rican and U.S. baseball fans alike remember Roberto Clemente (1934–1972) as one of the best baseball players ever. During his career, he led the Pittsburgh Pirates to two World Series wins. In 1966 he was named the U.S. National Baseball League's Most Valuable Player. Puerto Ricans also respect Clemente for donating his time and money to charities. In honor of his generosity, the Puerto Rican government, the U.S. National Baseball League, and others raised money to build the Roberto Clemente Sports City in Carolina, Clemente's hometown. Built in 1973, the center provides Puerto Rican kids with a place to play sports and make art.

Can you feel the beat? Salsa bands always get crowds on their feet.

Shake, Shake, **Shake!**

The Puerto Rican music and dance scenes are hopping. Music streams from stores, booms from car radios, and blares from loudspeakers. Radio stations play classical music and pop, rock, and rap songs, too.

Salsa is the spicy dance music of Puerto Rico. Musicians blend African and Caribbean rhythms with big-band jazz. A salsa band includes several singers, a piano, a bass (a large stringed instrument), trumpets, trombones, and saxophones. Other musicians shake maracas (rattles), tap cowbells, and beat bongos and congas (two kinds of drums). Put it all together and you've got music with fast rhythms, happy horns, and lots of smiling people. Puerto Rican–born Tito Puente is one of the most popular creators of salsa music.

Well-known classical musician Pablo Casals attracted Puerto Ricans to classical music. He played the cello, a large stringed instrument with a beautiful, rich sound. He moved from Spain to Puerto Rico in 1956 and helped to form the Puerto Rico Symphony Orchestra. The Pablo Casals Music Festival held every year in San Juan honors the memory of this fine musician.

Talented classical musicians please listeners at the Pablo Casals Music Festival.

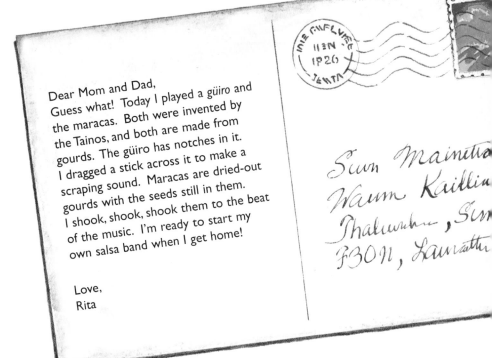

Dear Mom and Dad,
Guess what! Today I played a güiro and the maracas. Both were invented by the Tainos, and both are made from gourds. The güiro has notches in it. I dragged a stick across it to make a scraping sound. Maracas are dried-out gourds with the seeds still in them. I shook, shook, shook them to the beat of the music. I'm ready to start my own salsa band when I get home!

Love,
Rita

Tall **Tales**

Puerto Rico has inspired many writers and poets. Early authors wrote about the life of the settlers and about life under Spanish rule. Others have been inspired by Puerto Rico's mountains, landscape, and the mysteries of the rain forest. Modern writers tell tales about Puerto Ricans living in New York City and about the hardships of adjusting to a different way of life.

Both the Tainos and the Africans have rich histories of storytelling. In these cultures, folktales were passed down through the ages, with each storyteller adding his or her own details. Many legends explain why

Puerto Rico's rich landscape has provided the backdrop for many Puerto Rican stories.

animals look or act a certain way or how the world came to be. The Spaniards introduced fairytales with characters such as witches and princesses. One type of folktale unique to Puerto Rico tells about the life of the rural farmer called the jíbaro.

Puerto Ricans celebrate the jíbaro in stories and festivals.

Juan Bobo

One famous folktale character is Juan Bobo (Simple John). Juan is a jíbaro boy who often gets into trouble for not using his head. In one story, he dresses the family pig in his mother's best clothes and jewelry. In another he yells at a three-legged pot for being lazy, because with three legs, the pot should be able to walk faster than Juan Bobo.

39

A santero (left) **works carefully with a knife. To make mundillo, a weaver skillfully braids several bobbins (wooden spools wrapped with thread) back and forth to make an intricate pattern** (above).

Art for
Everyone

In all kinds of parades and celebrations, Puerto Ricans wear masks with faces of scary devils, animals, and imaginary creatures. Mask making is a well-known Puerto Rican art form, and it combines Taino, Spanish, and African crafts. Mask makers in Ponce and Loíza are famous for their creations.

Other artisans called *santeros* carve *santos* (saints) from wood. Santeros create detailed figures and religious scenes. Other Puerto Rican hand-made crafts include pottery and lace. Weavers shape *mundillo*, or beautiful handmade lace, into fancy ornaments.

One of Puerto Rico's fine artists, José Campeche, is known for his great paintings and for his clever use of materials. In the late 1700s, he created paints from local plants and flowers and used them to paint scenes on copper and wood.

Make a Mask

You will need:

a balloon

newspaper cut or ripped into strips
   about 12 inches long and ½ inch wide

egg carton cut into sections

masking tape

acrylic paint, sequins, construction paper,
   ribbons, and glue for decorating

paste:

½ cup flour

1 tablespoon salt

½ cup water

mixing bowl

wire whisk

Before you begin:

Ask an adult to help. This project can be messy. Cover your work surface with at least two layers of newspaper, then spread a plastic garbage bag over the paper.

To make the paste:

In a bowl, combine the flour and salt. Whisk in the water a little at a time until the paste becomes thick and creamy. Work out as many lumps as you can.

To make the mask:

1. Blow up and tie off the balloon.
2. Dip the newspaper strips, one at a time, into the paste, coating the paper thoroughly.
3. Over the paste bowl, run the coated strip between two fingers to remove excess paste.
4. Apply the strips the long way across the length of the balloon, overlapping them. Cover half of the balloon with four to five layers of newspaper strips. Let the mask dry until it hardens (24 to 36 hours).
5. With the masking tape, stick the egg carton sections, open end down, to the hardened form as eyes and a mouth. Make a fresh batch of paste and cover the egg cups with more strips of newspaper. Let dry.
6. Pop the balloon and peel it from the inside of the mold. Then you can paint your mask and decorate it with sequins, colored paper, and ribbons.

The opening to one of the caves at Río Camuy Cave Park looks like the entrance of a majestic cathedral.

Live It **Up!**

Most Puerto Ricans live in cities. Many hang out in parks in their spare time. Kids fly kites and play hopscotch. Girls gracefully skip double-Dutch jump rope. Boys and girls play computer and video games in arcades.

For a vacation, Puerto Ricans often head to the countryside. Many visit family and friends, while others explore parks, mountains, and beaches. The Río Camuy Cave Park is a popular vacation spot. The cave's entrance looks like carved sculpture. Underground rivers have gradually shaped the rock into beautiful forms. Spelunkers (cave explorers) can roam underground for miles.

The ocean offers hours of fun, too. Vacationers scuba dive in the deep, clear waters, surf the waves, and snorkel in the coves. At night, in certain warm bays, the water glitters when you stir it up. In the water live tiny one-celled animals that give off light. It's like an underwater fireworks show!

Surf's up! Puerto Rico's miles of beaches provide fun for people of all ages.

Horsing Around!

In the country, kids catch frogs or ride the famous *paso fino* horses. These horses are descendants from those brought to the island by Spanish settlers. Every March the town of Guayama hosts the Paso Fino Festival. People come from all over the country to watch the elegant horses compete. Paso fino horses are especially known for their gracefulness. A group of the horses runs wild on the island of Vieques.

43

Glossary

ancestor: A relative in the past, such as a great-great-great grandparent.

bilingual: Able to speak two different languages, such as Spanish and English, equally well.

cove: A shallow inlet or bay.

descendant: A person who came from an earlier person, family, or ethnic group. An individual descends directly from his or her parents, but a person's family tree can be traced to larger groups of long-ago relatives.

ethnic group: A large community of people that shares a number of social features, such as language, religion, or customs.

extended family: Mothers, brothers, sisters, grandparents, aunts, uncles, and cousins who may share one household.

foothills: A hilly region at the base of a mountain range.

hemisphere: One-half of the earth's surface. A globe, when divided vertically, shows the Western Hemisphere and the Eastern Hemisphere.

hurricane: A windstorm that begins over the ocean, picks up large amounts of rain, and can cause severe damage when striking land.

mangrove: A tropical tree that grows in wet saltwater areas.

plantation: A large land area used for growing one type of crop, such as bananas or cotton. Unskilled laborers typically work the land.

semidesert: An area of land sharing some characteristics of a desert, such as dry conditions and little rainfall. It often lies between a desert and a grassy area.

Beautiful San Juan is an attractive vacation spot for travelers from around the world.

tropical rain forest: A dense, green forest that receives large amounts of rain every year. These forests lie near the equator.

U.S. commonwealth: A territory that was once ruled by the United States and is still under its control to some degree.

Pronunciation Guide

Arecibo	(ah-ray-SEE-boh)
asopao	(ah-soh-POW)
Bayamón	(bah-yah-MOHN)
bayetes	(bah-YAY-tays)
Bienvenidos al Puerto Rico	(byehn-vay-NEE-dohs ahl PWAYR-toh REE-koh)
Borinquén	(boh-reen-KAYN)
Caguas	(CAH-gwahs)
Cerro de Punta	(SAY-roh day POON-tah)
colmado	(cohl-MAH-doh)
Cordillera Central	(cohr-dee-YAY-rah cehn-TRAHL)
Culebra	(coo-LAY-brah)
el coquí	(ehl koh-KEE)
el jíbaro	(ehl HEE-bah-roh)
El Yunque	(ehl YOON-kay)
espiritismo	(ays-pee-ree-TEES-moh)
Guayama	(gwah-YAH-mah)
güiro	(GWEE-roh)
Juan Bobo	(WAHN BOH-boh)
La Borinqueña	(lah boh-reen-KAYN-yah)
Luis Muñoz Rivera	(loo-EES moon-YOHS ree-VAY-rah)
Mayagüez	(my-ah-GWAYS)
mundillo	(moon-DEE-yoh)
Nuyorican	(noo-yoh-REE-kahn)
Ponce	(POHN-say)
San Juan	(SAHN WAHN)
santeros	(sahn-TAY-rohs)
Sierra de Luquillo	(SYAY-rah day loo-KEE-yoh)
Taino	(TY-noh)
tostones	(tohs-TOHN-ays)
Vieques	(VYAY-kays)

Further Reading

Aliotta, Jerome J. *The Puerto Rican Americans.* New York: Chelsea House Publishers, 1995.

Fradin, Dennis Brindel. *Puerto Rico.* Danbury, CT: Grolier Publications, 1998.

Kaufman, Cheryl. *Cooking the Caribbean Way.* Minneapolis: Lerner Publications Company, 1988.

Kent, Debora. *Puerto Rico.* Danbury, CT: Children's Press, 1991.

Márquez, Herón. *Destination San Juan.* Minneapolis: Lerner Publications Company, 1999.

Puerto Rico in Pictures. Minneapolis: Lerner Publications Company, 1995.

Puerto Rico. Minneapolis: Lerner Publications Company, 1994.

Temko, Florence. *Traditional Crafts from the Caribbean.* Minneapolis: Lerner Publications Company, 2000.

Walker, Paul Robert. *Pride of Puerto Rico: The Life of Roberto Clemente.* Orlando, FL: Harcourt Brace & Co., 1998.

Winslow, Zach. *Puerto Rico.* New York: Chelsea House Publishers, 1998.

Metric Conversion Chart

WHEN YOU KNOW:	MULTIPLY BY:	TO FIND:
teaspoon	5.0	milliliters
Tablespoon	15.0	milliliters
cup	0.24	liters
inches	2.54	centimeters
feet	0.3048	meters
miles	1.609	kilometers
square miles	2.59	square kilometers
degrees Fahrenheit	5/9 (after subtracting 32)	degrees Celsius

Index